Original title:
Sprigs of Inspiration

Copyright © 2025 Creative Arts Management OÜ
All rights reserved.

Author: Simon Fairchild
ISBN HARDBACK: 978-1-80567-381-1
ISBN PAPERBACK: 978-1-80567-680-5

Enlivened Visions

In a garden of daydreams, seeds will sprout,
Silly thoughts dance, there's no doubt!
A chicken in glasses, a cat with a hat,
Each giggle and chuckle, so much fun at that.

Pants that can talk and shoes that will sing,
Marshmallows floating on a bright, fluffy wing!
Tickling the daisies, joking with trees,
While squirrels tell secrets to the buzzing bees.

A rabbit that juggles, a frog that plays chess,
It's all quite absurd, but no need to stress!
Paint splashes colors, splats here and there,
Art with a wink, full of giggles to share.

So let's paint our dreams with laughter and cheer,
With each silly twist, bring the fun near!
For in this wild world where humor takes flight,
Every whimsy we nurture makes the day bright!

Mornings of Bright Potential

The coffee pot's a bubbling hell,
My hair looks like a failed spell.
I dance to tunes of morning glee,
While breakfast chases after me.

The sun peeks in like a tiny tease,
My toast pops up, but I just sneeze.
With butter flying across the room,
I'm ready now to face my doom.

Roots of Insight

I tried to plant a garden fair,
But ended up with weeds—oh, where?
The carrots claimed they needed light,
While cabbage laughed at my plight.

Fertilizer mixed with dreams,
Turned out worse than it all seems.
Nature giggles, watching me,
As I wrestle with this mystery.

Whimsy Under the Stars

Under the stars, my friends unwind,
With stories that are quite unrefined.
A pizza flies, it does a spin,
And laughter erupts, where do we begin?

Conversations bloom like summer's night,
In shades of giggles, pure delight.
The cosmos dances, winks and sways,
As we dream up nonsense 'til the rays.

Enchanted Growth

In my garden, wild things grew,
A pumpkin sprouted—who knew?
It overshadows every flower,
And mocks me hourly with its power.

I tend my plants with half a glance,
Yet they insist on having their dance.
With every sprout comes a big surprise,
I'm the gardener of empty pies!

Petals of Creativity

In the garden of ideas, I trip and fall,
Where thoughts bloom wildly, a laugh is in thrall.
I pluck a few petals, my hands get all sticky,
I write funny tales, and they seem rather picky.

A flower called nonsense, it danced in the breeze,
Swaying to rhythms that tickle like teasing.
With laughter like sunshine, it melts my gray mind,
In this petal parade, no dullness I find.

The Evergreen Spark

In the woods of whimsy, a spark did ignite,
A tree full of giggles, it tickled my fright.
Branches of laughter, leaves rustle with cheer,
Where squirrels tell jokes that I strangely hold dear.

Beneath its green canopy, jokes hang like fruit,
I reach for a quip and my worries go mute.
The roots of my humor run deep in the ground,
In this forest of giggles, my joy knows no bound.

Fragments of Daydreams

In my mind's little corners, bright sparks race around,
They bounce off each other, creating a sound.
A giggle, a snicker, a snort here and there,
All emojis of laughter in my dream's airy lair.

I catch these odd bits, like butterflies sweet,
They flutter and fumble, oh, aren't they a treat?
I paste them together, a collage of fun,
In this weird world of whimsy, I'm never outdone.

Threads of Imagination

With yarn made of giggles, I weave in delight,
A tapestry spun with the quirkiest sight.
Each thread tells a story, absurd and unique,
Creating sweaters where silliness peaks.

I knit all my visions, a scarf full of quirks,
Each stitch brings a chuckle as laughter berserks.
In the closet of whimsy, fashion takes flight,
With threads of my fancies, I strut day and night.

Twinkles of Originality

A wobbly chair sings out of tune,
A cat dances wildly, wearing a moon.
The fridge hums secrets, quite absurd,
While socks debate if they've flown with a bird.

A toaster dreams of flights on a plane,
While the sneakers argue, who's using whose brain?
With each silly thought, a chuckle will grow,
Who knew imagination had such a glow?

Flourishes of the Soul

An umbrella that wants to be a hat,
Joins forces with a table that claims it's a cat.
Together they plot to outwit a spoon,
While the clock giggles softly: 'Too soon, too soon!'

A pickle wearing boots saunters by,
Telling tall tales of how it can fly.
With sips of lemonade, laughter flows free,
In this garden of whimsy, come join in with me!

Murmurs of the Heart

A goldfish in pajamas whispers of dreams,
While the couch cushions hatch their grand schemes.
Pineapples giggle, decked out in flair,
As they navigate tangles of jellybean hair.

A toaster pops poetry, all burnt and crisp,
Reminiscing sweet moments, a soft, golden lisp.
Each chuckle brings light to an ordinary scene,
A world filled with nonsense, and a whole lot of green.

Glimmers of Hope

A squishy pie juggles with eyes full of cheer,
While chairs hold a party, all wishing to steer.
The sun winks at shadows playing tag on the wall,
As giggles erupt in the splendor of fall.

A punchline sits nestled in the crook of a tree,
Cracking up branches in shared jubilee.
With every hearty laugh, the day's troubles cease,
In a world where silliness grants moments of peace.

Harvesting Dreams

In the garden where dreams grow,
Pick them fresh, but take it slow.
Each silly thought, a ripe surprise,
Like chasing pigeons in blue skies.

We plant our wishes in the ground,
Hoping laughter will abound.
But tangled roots can cause a mess,
Like wearing socks with sandals—yes!

Twinkling Ideas at Twilight

At twilight's glow, ideas dance,
In my mind, they prance and prance.
With glitter hats and shoes so bright,
They tickle me, what a delight!

One jester thought, it jumps with glee,
It says, 'Why not a dog on a tree?'
I chuckle so, I can't contain,
The midnight snack that blocks my brain.

Radiant Seeds of Imagination

Seeds are sown in cloudy minds,
With rain of giggles, they're so kind.
They sprout up jokes and silly games,
Like llamas in top hats with names.

Each wacky thought needs room to bloom,
In this funny, wobbly room.
Watch as they burst into a show,
With every wink, they steal the glow.

Heartstrings and Blossoms

Heartstrings pull with a tug of fun,
As blossoms burst like a water gun.
Flowers laugh with colors bright,
Chasing butterflies in sheer delight.

String your heart like a bouncy ball,
Watch it bounce, don't let it fall.
In the garden of giggles, you'll find,
A playful soul, forever unconfined.

Tides of Potential

In a sea of ideas, I found a wave,
Riding on giggles, like a playful knave.
Sailing on thoughts that flip and flail,
Waves of nonsense that never grow stale.

With every splash, a quirky thought,
Like a fish on a bicycle, wildly fought.
Surfing the chaos, I cast my line,
Reeling in laughter, oh, how divine!

Dancing on bubbles, I feel so bright,
Chasing the tides, from morning to night.
Each ripple's a story, a laugh, a cheer,
Diving deep into the sea of my peers.

Fronds of Expression

Amidst the ferns, I twirl around,
With every leaf that flutters down.
Swaying and laughing, what a delight,
Even the lawn gnomes join in the fight.

Whimsical weeds whisper to me,
Tickling my toes, oh, can't you see?
With each sprout, a tale unfolds,
In this garden of giggles, joy behold!

Dancing with daisies, a floral jig,
Who knew that plants could be so big?
Growing with laughter, it's quite the show,
Each petal a punchline, watch them go!

Nestlings of Creativity

Little birds chirp in a frenzy of fun,
Building their nests, oh, what a run!
Doodles and scribbles in fluffy gray,
Each crack of a shell says 'Let's play!'

Peeking through branches, a curious sight,
Feathers and giggles take off in flight.
With every tweet, a new idea grows,
Chasing the sun where enchantment flows.

In the nest of thoughts, who wouldn't know,
A cacophony of laughter with every crow?
In this cozy chaos, we all belong,
Nestling our dreams, where we sing our song!

Brushstrokes of Enlightenment

With a splash of color, I dance on the page,
Every stroke a giggle, like a playful sage.
Painting my thoughts in a whimsical hue,
Swirling with capers, a vibrant view.

Dabbling in joy, I toss in a grin,
Mixing my colors, let the laughter begin.
From the palette of life, I brush and I play,
Crafting a canvas that's silly and gay.

Each stripe a story, a chuckle or two,
Exploring the mess while I'm splattering blue.
The muse on my shoulder dances with flair,
Creating a masterpiece beyond compare!

Melodies in Petal Form

Petals dance in breezy cheer,
A flower's tune, oh so near.
Bees buzz with a brand new song,
Swirling chaos, can't be wrong.

Colors clash like socks in drawers,
Nature's hum, it softly roars.
Who knew blooms could carry a beat?
With every bloom, humor's sweet.

They wiggle, sway, and tease aloof,
Like clowns beneath a leafy roof.
Pollen notes fill the sunny air,
Giggles burst from petals rare.

Amidst the leaves, life plays a game,
Bouncing, bouncing, who's to blame?
In every green, a wink and grin,
Nature's joke, where laughs begin.

Serene Moments of Clarity

In quiet times when thoughts collide,
A cat naps close, oh what a ride!
Sipping tea with crumbs so grand,
Ideas dance like grains of sand.

The kettle hums a silly tune,
I swear it thinks it's a raccoon.
Whiskers twitch, a thoughtful gaze,
Wondering if it's lost its ways.

Cherries roll on the windowsill,
Each one a thought, about to spill.
Oh, the joy of a random spark,
Like a firefly in the dark.

Fruits of thought, they tumble proud,
Under a sky so blissfully loud.
In the chaos, I find my zen,
Who knew clarity was a fun trend?

The Charms of Solitude

Alone but never lonely here,
Ice cream talks, it's perfectly clear.
A sock puppet shares its dreams,
Together we plot our silly schemes.

Tea parties with walls and chairs,
They gossip like the best of flares.
Bubbles float in a quirky dance,
Why not give the dust a chance?

Birds chirp in a gossiping spree,
They mock my hair, oh let it be!
A ballet of shadows plays on walls,
Whispers echo in empty halls.

In solitude, I find my flair,
Grocery lists, a witty affair.
Laughter rings where silence looms,
A world alive in my broom's fumes.

Flickers of Originality

Crayons scrawl ideas so bright,
Indigo dreams take off in flight.
With every squiggle, sparks ignite,
Originality, what a sight!

Doodles done with intent and grace,
A potato wears a smiling face.
Potatoes sigh, wishing for fame,
A life in art, oh what a game!

Ideas leap like frogs on springs,
In paper boats made of odd things.
Drifting through a sea of thought,
Inventive whims cannot be bought.

Noodle sculptures rule the land,
Spaghetti dreams at my command.
In every mess, a gem revealed,
Creativity's laugh, forever sealed.

Harmony in Nature's Embrace

The squirrel wears an acorn hat,
And prances like a little brat.
The flowers giggle, oh what fun,
As bees buzz round, a busy run.

The trees sway like they're dancing bold,
With whispers of secrets, yet untold.
A rabbit hops in mismatched shoes,
Spreading joy, while chasing blues.

The pond reflects a smiling sun,
Where frogs croak out their wacky pun.
Nature's stage, an endless play,
With quirks that brighten up the day.

Amidst this goofy, green parade,
Life's little joys will never fade.
In laughter, roots grow deep and wide,
In nature's charm, we all abide.

Awakening the Dreamer

A snail with dreams of flying high,
Wears shades beneath the sunny sky.
The ladybug claims she can dance,
Flipping on leaves, a daring chance.

In gardens where the daisies giggle,
A caterpillar starts to wiggle.
"A butterfly?" says every bee,
"We'll be the judges; wait and see!"

The worms hold workshops under ground,
Sharing tips on how to spin around.
While butterflies stop for tea and cake,
In this sweet realm, a life they make.

The stars twinkle with great delight,
As dreamers dance through the night.
With every whim and wild surprise,
Excitement twirls in gentle sighs.

A Canvas of Fresh Perspectives

With a paintbrush made of twigs and leaves,
The clouds create what nature weaves.
Sunbeams spill like laughter bright,
As shadows play, a cheeky sight.

The mountains wink with snow-capped crowns,
While valleys stretch their leafy gowns.
The rivers chuckle, twisted and free,
As they tickle the stones with glee.

Dandelions puff with sassy flair,
Sprouting wishes in the air.
Each petal flutters with cute designs,
Nature's humor, in playful lines.

The world's a canvas, wild and bold,
With tales of whimsy, yet untold.
Brush your dreams with colors bright,
Let laughter echo in pure delight.

Echoes in the Green

Amidst the leaves, a chorus sings,
With chirps and chuckles, what joy it brings.
A woodpecker taps a funny beat,
While rabbits sway on tiny feet.

The whispers of grass tickle the toes,
As earthworms share delightful woes.
The daisies roll their petals wide,
Hoping the ants will join the ride.

In the shade, a wise old owl,
Cackles softly, gives a growl.
"Life's a hoot," he says with pride,
As squirrels join his joyful stride.

In nature's heart, so light and free,
Echoes of laughter create harmony.
Live it up, let worries flee,
In the green world, be just as glee.

The Breath of Innovation

Ideas dance like wild cats,
Stirring up thoughts in silly hats.
A quirky twist, a mind so bright,
Sparks fly on this whimsical flight.

Bouncing balls of laughter roam,
In the land of thought, they call it home.
Each brainstorm's a jester in disguise,
With antics that leave us in surprise.

Inventions that wobble and wobble some more,
Like a chicken with shoes, it's hard to ignore!
With giggles and guffaws, we blend our ideas,
In this carnival of creativity, cheering with cheers.

Nature's Caress

A leaf fell down with a jaunty jig,
Whispering secrets, so bold and big.
Squirrels giggle, chasing their tails,
While flowers gossip in the soft gales.

The sun winks down, a playful glare,
While clouds play hide-and-seek in midair.
Nature's a prankster with tricks up her sleeve,
Plucking ideas from the web that we weave.

Bees buzz in rhymes, seemingly absurd,
Engaging in chatter with every heard word.
A symphony of chuckles from every tree,
Is nature hiding laughter? Let it be free!

Chasing the Inkwell

With pens like swords, we duel with ink,
Ideas flow faster than you can think.
Characters plot with mischief in stride,
While plot twists dance like they're on a ride.

A poet's quill scribbles all night,
In search of the words that take flight.
Ink stains on fingers, a badge of pride,
Each page a treasure where dreams reside.

Comical twists where laughter takes charge,
Oh look! A giraffe playing at large.
As we chase that elusive well,
Join the fun, only time will tell!

Dreamcatcher Leaves

Leaves spin gently on an autumn breeze,
Catching dreams like spiders, oh such expertise!
Hilarious visions of dancing frogs,
A symphony of joy in the wakes of fogs.

Catching dreams, they twirl and glide,
Like juggling squirrels on a wild ride.
With each little twist, a giggle released,
In this playful web, the laughter increased.

The moon's a joker, winking and bright,
Guiding our dreams through the velvety night.
So toss your worries, let cherubs weave,
In this funny realm, there's always reprieve!

Sips of Clarity

A cup of coffee with a smile,
Makes thoughts collide, it's worth the while.
Creamy dreams swirl in the brew,
Frothy ideas, all bright and new.

A sip of tea, oh what a thrill,
Helps me ponder, helps me chill.
With every gulp, my mind takes flight,
Who knew caffeine could feel so right?

Lemonade with a twist of fate,
Got me pondering at a rapid rate.
Ice cubes clink like lightbulbs' spark,
Sudden epiphanies in the park.

A fizzy soda, bubbles rise,
Each pop and hiss a sweet surprise.
With laughter bubbling like the drink,
I muse and ponder faster than you think.

Notes of a Serene Mind

A pencil dances across my page,
Jokes and quips, thoughts set to stage.
I write a ballad about my cat,
Wearing a hat, how silly is that?

As clouds parade in the bright blue sky,
A rubber duck floats by and waves hi.
My thoughts become silly like a game,
Plucking notes that won't bring me shame.

A serenade sung to a loaf of bread,
Every crumb whispers things left unsaid.
A laugh erupts from my scribbled plight,
Who knew loaves could giggle with delight?

The peaceful hum of a quiet day,
Writes itself in a cheeky way.
Serenity spins like a whirligig,
Chasing thoughts that dance and jig.

Whispers of the Muse

A tickle under my sleepy nose,
The muse is here, and goodness knows!
She tells me tales of whimsical things,
Like a hedgehog wearing tiny blings.

In the quiet nook where ideas sprout,
She plucks a thought with a giggly shout.
"Let's write of socks that lost their way,
Or a donut who wished to dance today!"

With every whisper, the pages jive,
As unicorns come alive and thrive.
Each silly rhyme a treasured surprise,
Invisible ink in my laughter cries.

So I chase her shadow on this light breeze,
Crafting verses with giggles and ease.
A dance of delight, a poetic ruse,
With my best friend, the ever-witty muse.

Blooming Thoughts at Dawn

As sunlight tickles a sleepy face,
A garden of ideas finds its place.
Petals of humor burst into bloom,
In the morning's light, there's plenty of room.

With dew drops glistening on a leaf,
I ponder jokes beyond belief.
A sunflower winks, "Why so glum?"
"Because I tripped on a bumblebee's drum!"

Butterflies flutter with giggles and grace,
They tease the flowers, "Join the race!"
A daisy shouts, "Don't peep too loud,
We're all silly, let's make a crowd!"

With every laugh, the world awakes,
In this flora, humor spins and shakes.
A bloom of joy in the light of dawn,
Turns frowns to smiles—no need for a con.

Radiance Unfurled

In the garden of giggles, where daisies dance,
The sun wears a hat, takes a jolly chance.
Worms sing in harmony, they tickle the toes,
While butterflies compete in their fanciest clothes.

A squirrel on stilts takes a hop and a twirl,
Demanding attention, he gives it a whirl.
The tomatoes are laughing, it's quite a parade,
While cabbage plays maracas, totally unafraid.

Bees buzz with laughter, they bump and they bounce,
While roses crack jokes, and the thorns play pounce.
Each petal a mask, they wear with delight,
In this wacky garden, everything feels right.

So here's to the cheer, let's dance with delight,
In this garden of giggles, everything's bright!
Where humor and flowers go hand in hand,
And nature's a jester, across this wild land.

Colors of the Muse

With crayons of laughter, we paint the day,
Each stroke a chuckle, in a funny way.
The blue skies giggle, as clouds wear a grin,
While rainbows tickle us from where they begin.

Purple paisleys on jackets, what a sight to behold,
Fashion of whimsy, the colors are bold.
A dapper old cat struts, sporting a tie,
While canaries in hats sing songs to the sky.

In this palette of nonsense, where silliness reigns,
Each hue tells a joke, and humor remains.
A banana peel slides, oh don't take a fall,
As we leap into laughter, let's share it with all.

So gather your brushes, paint joy all around,
With colors of laughter, let's turn it up sound.
In this canvas of quirky, where giggles don't lose,
We find our true essence, in colors of muse.

Breezes of Change

The wind brings a chuckle, with giggles in tow,
As trees start to wiggle, in the light breeze flow.
Leaves shaking hands with the clouds up above,
Spreading the laughter, like a warm, gentle shove.

A kite takes a tumble, it's flopping about,
While kids laugh and cheer, never feeling doubt.
The daisies are swaying, having a ball,
As the breeze whispers secrets, a laugh for us all.

With every gust blowing, the humor grows rich,
Even the old fences get in on the pitch.
The post starts to shimmy, the grass tries to dance,
Inviting all who see, to join in the chance.

So when the wind giggles, and the world feels a shift,
Let's embrace all the fun, life's magical gift.
With breezes of laughter, everything's grand,
As we twirl with the wind, hand in hand.

Hidden Treasures in Bloom

In the backyard jungle, where secrets reside,
We peek at the bushes, colorful and wide.
A gnome with a wink, and a smile quite grand,
Tells tales of the treasures hid under the sand.

The daisies are gossiping, spreading the news,
While mischievous rabbits wear sparkly shoes.
A daffodil whispers, the truth in a rhyme,
That sometimes the best laughs come out of the grime.

With quirks hidden deeply, we dig and we find,
A treasure of laughter, in blossoms entwined.
The weeds play the jester, while daisies play queen,
In this blooming kingdom, there's no need to preen.

So wander the gardens, where surprises abound,
With petals of humor, let joy be profound.
In this wild patch of giggles, let's bloom and take flight,
Finding treasures of laughter, shining so bright.

Whispers of Fresh Beginnings

A squirrel with a bowtie, oh what a sight,
Dancing on rooftops, under the moonlight.
He's planning a party, with nuts on the floor,
Inviting the raccoons to come and explore.

With a wink and a jig, they gather and cheer,
Each one with a snack, bringing joy and good beer.
Laughter erupts, it's a furry delight,
Who knew fresh starts could be such a sight?

Out of the bushes, a rabbit hops in,
Declaring a contest to see who can spin.
He flips and he flops, with great pomp and flair,
While everyone giggles, they just don't care.

So here's to the critters, their raucous parade,
In the world of beginnings, mischief is made.
Join in their fun, let your worries all sway,
Life's just a dance in this comedic display.

Petals of Possibility

In a garden of chaos, the flowers all scheme,
They whisper and giggle, it's a wild dream.
Tulips in tutus, sunflowers with shades,
Creating a ballet, in the soft glades.

The daisies debate, who can twirl the best?
While lilacs debate, on who's truly blessed.
A bumblebee joins, with a tune oh so sweet,
Buzzing along, he can't help but tap his feet.

Laughter is blooming, in every bright hue,
Petals all pulse with the joy of the crew.
They plan a parade, with sprinkles and cake,
In a world full of blooms, all the rules they'll break.

As twilight approaches, their mischief ignites,
In a giggly explosion of colorful sights.
So grab your own blooms, let giggles abound,
In this garden of fun, where joy knows no bound.

Echoes of Creative Dawn

Morning arrives on a wave of a laugh,
With paintbrushes dancing, it's a quirky craft.
A toaster is singing, a kettle's in tune,
While cereal spoons are juggling by noon.

The fridge joins the chorus, with magnets that cheer,
Each item a note, in this symphonic sphere.
Eggs flip like acrobats, toast takes a bow,
As pancakes twirl, in a synchronized wow!

In each playful echo, creativity soars,
From the cat in a beret, to the dog with a score.
They plot an adventure, a treasure to find,
With maps made of napkins, and dreams intertwined.

So rise with the sun, let your laughter arise,
In this dawn of delight, wear your joy as a prize.
Join the cacophony, let your spirit awake,
In this cheerful ballet, all your worries will break.

Fragments of a New Vision

A pirate with glasses, a parrot named Dave,
Set sail on a gelato, a tasty little wave.
They searched for lost treasures, beneath whipped cream skies,
Where sprinkles are coins and the seagulls all rise.

With a map made of cookies and gumdrop delight,
They navigated puddles, while taking a bite.
The captain declared, "This is life's sweetest game!"
As the crew all cheered, calling out each name.

A mermaid appeared, with glitter and flair,
Offering seashells from her magical lair.
She joined in the fun, throwing rainbows for free,
As laughter erupted, like waves from the sea.

So join in the adventure, let out your own grin,
In this whimsical world, where the fun can begin.
With pirates and mermaids, laughter is clear,
Fragments of joy that will always endear.

Veils of Aspiration

In the depths of my daydreams, I trip on my thoughts,
My hopes wear a cape, but just tie themselves in knots.
Chasing a vision that sparkles and spins,
While I wrestle with puzzles that tickle my chins.

A ladder to nowhere, I climb with a sneeze,
Each stubbed toe an omen, or so it could tease.
My goals play hide and seek, and I join in the fun,
But all I've uncovered is my old gum from '91.

The clouds paint my story, in shades of pure pink,
While my cat judges my efforts with an epitaph wink.
I chuckle at missteps that tumble like dust,
The road to my triumphs, made sticky with crust.

So here's to the moments that make us all laugh,
Like stepping on rakes, in a bright photograph.
With dreams like balloons, floating up in the breeze,
I'll gather the giggles, and dance with the trees.

Flickers of Bright Ideas

A lightbulb popped on, but it's hanging by a string,
Like a bat on a branch that forgot how to swing.
My brainstorms spray paint in colors too loud,
While my good sense retreats, hiding under a cloud.

I scribble mad wishes on napkins and walls,
My thoughts swirling like confetti in grand festival balls.
But wisdom is shy, it plays tag on the run,
As I chase after thoughts like my dog with a bun.

Oh, the quirks of invention are winks in disguise,
Like a hamster in sunglasses, too cool for the wise.
I giggle at concepts that bounce on my brain,
Wishing for sanity—alas! That's in vain!

So let's raise our glasses to ideas that bumble,
To crafting and chaos and all of life's fumble.
With a wink and a laugh, I'll sketch a new plot,
Finding joy in the nonsense, it's the best I've got!

Gardens of the Mind

In the backyard of thinking, where wild thoughts grow,
Rumors of brilliance are spread by a crow.
The weeds of distraction entwine with my plans,
While sunflowers giggle, saying, 'There go the fans!'

I plant seeds of nonsense, they sprout in a line,
Watered with coffee, caffeine's my sunshine.
The zucchini of wisdom rolls off to the side,
While my carrot of logic has taken a ride.

Bees buzz with gossip, they're working so hard,
While snails on a mission are fetching my card.
The tomatoes of fortune are juicily ripe,
But I'm chasing the squash with a leap and a hype!

So here in my garden, I dance with delight,
As squirrels mull my plans over nuts for a bite.
With laughter and quirks, I'll prune what I find,
For blooming in chaos is the fate of the mind.

Currents of Innovation

Riding the waves of what could be the next,
I paddle my dreams on a board made of text.
With a splash and a giggle, my thoughts take a dive,
As I chase after currents where wild ideas thrive.

I build boats of nonsense, they float on a breeze,
With sails made of candy and hulls made of cheese.
Adventure's a seagull that steals my cornbread,
While I navigate storms that swirl in my head.

In the sea of the future, I flop like a fish,
While jellyfish ideas float by on a wish.
But the tide brings me laughter, it's never so grim,
As I surf through the zany, with whimsy in swim.

So toast to the creatives who ride with a grin,
In the waters of whimsy, let the fun begin!
With paddles of humor, let's splash with delight,
Innovations await in this whimsical flight.

Kaleidoscope of Ideas

When thoughts collide, they spin and dance,
A jumbled mix that leaves a chance.
Colors swirl in wild delight,
As nonsense takes to glorious flight.

The cat wears shoes, the dog can sing,
A parrot dresses up like a king.
Ideas tumble, plop, and flop,
In this zany mind, they never stop.

UFOs play hopscotch in the sky,
While talking toasters toast with a sigh.
Jumping beans have got some moves,
Creativity grooves, and laughter soothes.

So grab your hat and join the ride,
In this silly world, laughter won't hide.
Sketch a dream, or paint a frown,
In the kaleidoscope, you'll never drown.

The Garden of Dreams

In the garden where daffodils giggle,
Lettuce waltzes, and tomatoes wiggle.
The gnomes converse in riddles and rhymes,
While the carrots dance, keeping perfect times.

Cucumbers wear hats all day long,
Radishes sing an off-key song.
The sunflowers sway with a silly grace,
Cheering up plants with a smiling face.

Butterflies host silly tea parties,
As the bees join in, sweet and artsy.
With honeyed laughter lingering near,
Dreams grow wild in this garden so dear.

So plant a thought, let it sprout,
In the garden where giggles are about.
With every bloom, let joy's melody chime,
In this whimsical place, we'll have a good time.

Harvesting Inner Light

In fields of laughter, we sow the seeds,
Planting ideas like tiny weeds.
With a basket of joy, we dance around,
Harvesting chuckles from the quirky ground.

The moon gives advice, ever so wise,
While starlit whispers make us rise.
With wiggly worms, we share a chat,
Our thoughts flutter like a silly hat.

The sun pulls pranks, with shadows to cast,
As giggles and glee sweep through so fast.
We gather the light, so warm and bright,
Bottling laughter, pure and alight.

So pick a thought, let it shine,
In the fields of silly, it's all divine.
With each little quirk, let joy take flight,
As we harvest moments wrapped in light.

Tapestry of Visions

Weaving dreams with threads so bold,
Each pattern crafted, a story told.
With giggles stitched in every seam,
This tapestry's woven from the silliest dream.

A dragon rides a bike so bright,
While unicorns twirl in pure delight.
The colors clash but cheer so loud,
In this madcap quilt, we all feel proud.

Spinning yarns like cotton candy,
Each twist and turn, so soft and dandy.
With punny phrases and wacky tales,
This woven wonder never fails.

So come and see this vibrant thread,
Where humor lives, and joy is spread.
In the tapestry of life, hold tight,
For in every stitch, there's pure delight.

Inspiration Unleashed

Ideas tumble down like rain,
Splat! A thought—oh, what a gain!
A noodle here, a wiggly fry,
Mix 'em up, and off we fly!

Chasing squirrels in my head,
One holds a book, the other—bread!
Frantic thoughts, a merry dance,
I laughed so hard, I lost my pants!

Puns and giggles, all around,
Building castles from the ground.
Colorful birds in a silly spree,
Painting the world, just wait and see!

Whimsical dreams like candy canes,
Writing rhymes that twist like trains.
Who knew inspiration could be so funny?
A punchline here, and oh—it's sunny!

The Pulse of Creativity

A bee buzzes loudly past my ear,
I grab a pen, fueled by cheer.
Spaghetti thoughts all twirled and curled,
A masterpiece! Why not? Let's whirl!

Rabbits in hats, juggling bright,
Ideas leap from left to right.
Tap dancing on a coffee cup,
Let's fill our minds, let's shake it up!

Bright crayons shatter, colors burst,
What's next? A unicorn or a cursed?
With each new sketch, I guffaw and grin,
Who knew creative chaos could win?

Beating drums, while odd socks pair,
Wrap your thoughts in lots of flair.
A roast chicken wearing a hat,
Is there a muse that's fun and fat?

Glistening Dreams

Puddles of laughter scatter wide,
Jellybeans dance—oh, what a ride!
Dreams sprinkled with glitter, oh so bright,
A parade of nonsense under the moonlight!

Twirling poodles in polka dots,
They trip and tumble, but I like their spots.
Each fumble feels like a happy play,
In this land of dreams, I want to stay!

Cookie dough clouds float high above,
Whisking up fluff, oh, what a love!
I skip on rainbows, giggles abound,
The best ideas are spun around!

With jellyfish singing silly tunes,
I join along, waving my spoons.
Glistening gems of joy in the air,
Every chuckle beckons a dare!

Wandering in the Meadow

In a meadow of giggles, I roam so free,
Chasing butterflies that laugh with me.
Each flower's shout, a joke on the breeze,
Nature's punchline amongst the trees!

Frogs wear crowns and dance with grace,
While squirrels giggle in a nutty race.
Acorns drop like falling stars,
Tickling my toes from nearby jars.

Clouds take shapes of whimsical pies,
I wonder—do they share our sighs?
I scribble notes on a leaf so green,
The silliest thoughts I've ever seen!

With every step, a snicker grows,
Finding joy in what life shows.
I'll gather laughter like wildflowers,
In this meadow of wondrous hours!

Embers of Passion

A spark ignites with every laugh,
Ideas bloom like daisies in a path.
Chasing thoughts like cats on a spree,
Silly notions dance, wild and free.

Coffee spills, oh what a mess,
Yet somehow we feel truly blessed.
With every blunder, joy does rise,
Fueling dreams under the sunny skies.

Tickles of wit bring light to the night,
Each failed attempt, a comedy so bright.
With charcoal dreams and goofy grins,
Who knew this madness could lead to wins?

So let's embrace this funky thrill,
With laughter as our secret skill.
In every fumble, a chance to soar,
With embers of passion, we'll ask for more!

Shadows of a Bright Idea

In the back of my mind, a thought did roam,
Wearing a hat, it found a home.
Dancing wildly with glee and grace,
A shadowed critter in a silly place.

With a wink and a grin, it takes a leap,
Tripping over giggles, it's not too deep.
It steals your pen, writes on the wall,
Whispers 'let's have fun,' but oh, what a brawl!

Ideas clash like rocks at sea,
Yet every splash brings back to me.
Lurking in corners, too shy to show,
Shadows invite us—come on, let's go!

In a world where nonsense meets the wise,
Each silly vision fertilizes.
From shadows rise the most absurd schemes,
Filling our hearts with wild, sweet dreams!

Crescendo of New Dreams

From whispers soft to roars of glee,
New dreams bubble up like a fizzy spree.
They tickle our minds, a raucous delight,
Juggling visions 'til the morning light.

With every chuckle, a new plot twist,
Creating a life that can't be missed.
A crescendo builds, with no need for stress,
For humor makes this world our best guess.

Flipping through ideas like pancakes so fine,
Each golden flip, a new chance to shine.
A riddle here or a pun on a lark,
In the symphony of joy, we find our spark.

Let's dance to the rhythm of laughter's tune,
As dreams explode like confetti at noon!
In the crescendo, let's frolic and play,
Creating chaos in the funniest way!

Waves of Unexpected Joy

Riding the tide with a goofy grin,
Unexpected moments just begin.
Like jellyfish bouncing on a sunny day,
We sway with laughter, come what may.

With every wave, a splash of cheer,
Tickles our spirits, making it clear.
Surprising turns like a twisty slide,
We catch the joy, let it be our guide.

Bubbles and giggles in the salty air,
In this ocean of fun, who has time to scare?
Every gull cackles, a comedic show,
With each wave crashing, we let worries go.

So let's surf on the crest of delight,
With hearts wide open and spirits bright.
Our journey's a riot, our laughter a tool,
Riding waves of joy, we make our own rule!

Rejuvenation in Full Bloom

In a garden of thoughts, I trip on my shoe,
The flowers are laughing, 'We knew you'd come through!'

Bees dance like they're training for a silly show,
While daisies gossip about the sun's weird glow.

The watering can glugs, spilling secrets of rain,
The tulips roll their eyes, 'There's no need to complain!'
A worm winks at me, wearing a leaf for a hat,
And somewhere a cactus is having a spat.

When petals burst forth with a zany delight,
The insects host parties that last through the night.
With splashes of color that make the day bright,
My garden's a circus, a comedic sight!

So here's to the blooms that tickle and tease,
They prank all the pollen and dance in the breeze.
In laughter and joy, our spirits ascend,
In this wild, vibrant Eden, where fun knows no end.

Branching Out: New Horizons

I climbed up a tree, thought I'd take a peek,
But branches below me began to squeak.
'The higher you go, the funnier it gets,'
Said a squirrel with sunglasses, placing his bets.

With each wriggle and sway, I spread wild my arms,
Pretending I'm flying, or charming with charms.
The leaves whispered loudly, 'You're such a big deal!'
While acorns conspired to steal my last meal.

A parrot flew by with a joke on its beak,
Totally lost in a comic mystique.
'What do you get when you plant a light bulb?'
'A hard light to follow, but dreams to engulf!'

Down below, the forest was laughing at me,
As I swayed to the rhythm of the unruly tree.
Branching out boldly, I'm tumbling and free,
Mood angles warped, but oh, joy's the key!

Ephemeral Insights

A cloud fluffs my thoughts like a mischievous ghost,
'What's that? An epiphany? Or just burnt toast?'
I scribble my whims on napkins galore,
As ideas take flight and then sneak out the door.

The sun peeks at me with a wink and a grin,
'You're grasping at straws, let the chaos begin!'
The wind hoots with laughter, rustling all joy,
Tossing my musings like a kite with a toy.

Each flicker of thought feels slippery and brief,
Like a banana peel hiding a comic relief.
Inspiration pops, like a bubble in soup,
As I chase each one with an exaggerated whoop!

In this comical chase, I find my true spark,
For in silly moments, we brighten the dark.
So here I'll remain, with my pen and some cheer,
To harness the laughter that dances so near.

Harvest of the Heart

I planted some giggles in a field of my mind,
And waited for chuckles to sprout out in kind.
With a fork and a trowel, I dug up a pun,
Just to find out, it wanted to run.

The carrots reveal that they're pulling a prank,
Twirling around like they're in some big tank.
With tomatoes conspiring to roll down the hill,
I laugh as I gather, my basket to fill.

A silly old scarecrow starts dancing with glee,
'Oh look! It's a harvest, come join in with me!'
I twirl with the squash as the breezes do blow,
Bouncing through laughter, letting merriment flow.

In this bountiful garden, joy seeds are the prize,
With kaleidoscopic dreams that twinkle and rise.
And who knew this harvest would fill up my heart,
With humor and whimsy, a truly fine art!

Flora of the Mind

In the garden where thoughts take flight,
Ideas sprout in the morning light.
Weeds of doubt, we pull them out,
While giggles echo throughout the route.

Blossoms bloom where laughter grows,
Nonsense whispers beneath our noses.
Petals dance like silly socks,
Wrapped in wordplay, tickling clocks.

With pollen bright, we spread our cheer,
Mixing giggles with a dash of beer.
Bees in bowties buzzing along,
As we compose this silly song.

In the sketches of our playful dreams,
We paint with colors, or so it seems.
Each stroke a joke, each shade a grin,
A garden of giggles we're planting within.

Dances of the Heart

Waltzing with thoughts, we skip and sway,
In the ballroom of life, come what may.
Two left feet in a tango of fun,
Spinning circles till the day is done.

Hearts doing the cha-cha, oh what a sight,
Giddy laughter in the pale moonlight.
Stomping on toes when the beat goes wrong,
Each misstep turns into a silly song.

Cotton candy on a whiskered face,
We break the rules of a dreary pace.
Twists and twirls like a jester's play,
Chasing worries, they scatter away.

From salsa shuffles to breakdance spins,
Let's dance together, where the fun begins.
In the rhythm of laughter, we find our way,
In this heart-to-heart where joy leads the sway.

Seeds of Wonder

Planting tiny dreams in a whimsical plot,
Watering each with a giggle and thought.
Sprouting odd ideas with a twist of fate,
In the sunshine of smiles, it's never too late.

Whimsical critters come out to play,
Telling tall tales in a silly bouquet.
Rabbits with glasses, all reading the news,
While dancing on top of their colorful shoes.

Bouncing bubbles of laughter arise,
As we harvest our hearts with sparkly eyes.
Each seed a joke, each sprout a pun,
In the field of wonder, we all become one.

With a sprinkle of joy and a dash of fun,
We gather together 'til the day is done.
In this garden of giggles, we nurture the small,
With seeds of wonder, we'll grow them all.

Vibrant Echoes

Echoes of laughter bounce off the walls,
In the corridors where fun calls.
With a silly billy and a cheeky grin,
We gather together, let the games begin.

Whispering rumors of a pie in the sky,
We roll on the floor as the moments fly by.
With ticklish tickles and jokes galore,
Our vibrant echoes just beg for more.

In the meadow of mischief where memories play,
We sketch out smiles in a colorful way.
Each giggle a note in this jovial tune,
In a symphony of sunshine beneath the moon.

Waves of whimsy sweep us along,
In the chorus of joy, we all belong.
Vibrant echoes dance in the night air,
In the laughter's embrace, we go anywhere.

Fables of Renewal

In a garden of socks, they grow,
The odd ones that no one would sow.
With a wink and a twist, they dance,
Turning laundry into a romanced chance.

A turtle takes lessons from a hare,
In a race where no one seems to care.
With mismatched shoes and hats askew,
They giggle at what no one knew.

The flowers wear glasses, all askew,
Listening to gossip from the dew.
Chasing away all the gloom,
While sunbeams paint each blossom room.

A snail's got a suitcase, can you believe?
He's packing for a trip on a leaf!
With sunhats and snacks, oh what a sight,
Off to explore at the speed of light!

Tangles of Hope

In a labyrinth of spaghetti, they dance,
The forks all in frenzy, they prance.
With meatballs as friends, they twirl around,
In sauce-covered joy, laughter is found.

A cat in a hat steals the show,
Mixing up colors, putting on a glow.
With whiskers decorated, so bold,
He's the jester in stories untold.

Cheese mice with dreams of a dance,
In sneakers too big, they take a chance.
Wobbling and bobbing, they take the floor,
Who knew little mice could be so hardcore?

A garden of dreams where the daisies play,
Organizing picnics every sunny day.
With ants as waiters, they set the scene,
Serving up sunshine, the food is pristine!

Vignettes of Joy

A frog in a suit, he's ready to roll,
With a top hat that's taking a stroll.
He croaks out a tune, a jazzy delight,
Making everyone laugh at his sight.

A penguin's lost in a pair of flip-flops,
Sliding and slipping, oh how he flops!
With a splash and a dash, he's the star of the day,
At the beach where he dares to play.

The sunbeams yodel, creating a cheer,
While squirrels juggle acorns, oh dear!
A party of nuts, it's a tapas affair,
Whisking away all your worry and care.

A butterfly joins the dance with style,
In shoes made of lace, she's full of guile.
With sparkles and giggles, up high she soars,
Spreading joy, leaving laughter galore!

Rays of Unwritten Stories

In a library where books can sing,
Librarians twirl as they take wing.
With pages that giggle and covers that grin,
Words fly about, let the fun begin!

A quokka with dreams on a rainbow slide,
In search of adventures, what a wild ride!
He bounces and bobs with a bright, cheeky smile,
Taking every challenge, oh what style!

A cactus in boots is dancing away,
Spinning in circles, he's out to play.
With prickly moves that defy all the rules,
He's the life of the party, showing off jewels.

Through clouds of laughter, new tales arise,
In a world of mischief, where fun never dies.
So grab a pen and jot down the score,
For every giggle opens a brand new door!

Dewdrops of Creativity

In a garden of thoughts, I found a pear,
I propped it on my head, quite the wild affair.
A squirrel giggled, his jokes so spry,
Who knew that nuts could make ideas fly?

A butterfly landed, quite close to my nose,
Tickled by whimsy, I struck a pose.
With paint on my fingers, I danced in the rain,
A masterpiece born from a splash and a stain.

Branches of Hope

Under a tree, with a cat and a hat,
I pondered the universe over snacks and a chat.
The breeze whispered secrets of giggles and dreams,
While squirrels debated on life's wacky schemes.

The branches above began to sway and spin,
I joined in the laughter, let the fun begin.
With sunshine as my muse, I danced around,
Turning every frown upside down with a sound.

Chasing Ethereal Shadows

In the twilight hush, I saw shadows race,
I chased them around, with a bemused face.
They tripped on my thoughts, which spiraled with glee,
Laughing at echoes, just shadows and me.

A ghostly figure waved, a prankster at heart,
Mischief unfolded, a true work of art.
When shadows roared laughter, I couldn't help but grin,
Guess the best ideas come when you let chaos win!

Blossoms of Serendipity

In a field of odd socks, flowers began to bloom,
Each petal a laughter, filling the room.
A daisy poked fun, the sun turned to giggle,
As bees formed a band and began to wiggle.

With candy-coated thoughts, I jumped in delight,
Twirling like cupcakes in the soft morning light.
Serendipity shines when mishaps unite,
Turning the ordinary into pure delight.

Blossoms of Thought

In a garden of goblins, thoughts sprout wide,
They wiggle and giggle, nowhere to hide.
A butterfly sneezes, it's such a delight,
Tickling daisies that dance day and night.

Every whimsy whispers, a riddle or two,
As toadstools debate on what's silly to chew.
Laughter blooms brightly amongst daffodils,
While a frog shares secrets on high-flying quills.

Silly tulips prance in a polka dot hat,
Juggling inspiration like a well-fed cat.
With each twist of humor that tickles the air,
The world's full of giggles, if only we care.

So come join the frolic, let your mind find a path,
In this bloom of tomfoolery, come share in the laugh!
For each thought that blossoms is bound to take flight,
And dance through the shadows, igniting delight.

Threads of Imagination

Weaving bright stories with threads of pure fun,
Where socks turn to monsters, and turtles can run.
A cat in a bow tie reads Shakespeare aloud,
While the fish in the tank cheers, feeling quite proud.

With imaginations that bounce all around,
A hamster in pajamas runs laps on the ground.
Bananas can sing, if you listen just right,
While chairs hold a meeting to discuss their plight.

The couch tells of dreams of a life in a park,
As the lamp in the corner giggles and sparks.
Each thread spun enchantment, a colorful chase,
In a world where the zany has found its own space.

So gather your wishes, your laughter, your schemes,
Let's stitch up a quilt made of whimsical dreams!
With needles of joy, we'll sew up a spree,
In this fabric of fancy, come dance wild and free!

Seeds of Change

Planting ideas like seeds in the breeze,
Mixing up notions like a salad with cheese.
Out pops a fish with a grin on its face,
As change taps its toes, keeping up with the pace.

Squirrels shout "Eureka!" from high in the trees,
With acorns containing most curious keys.
A cake made of rainbows, a pie filled with mirth,
Transforms all the stumps 'til they bounce with great girth.

So grab a bright seed and let giggles grow tall,
Beside a cheeky gorilla who's juggling a ball.
With each silly sprout, we'll dance in the sun,
As change becomes laughter, and we all join the fun!

Who knew that ideas could wiggle about,
In a patch full of chortles where joy has no doubt?
Let's plant all our wishes where whimsy can play,
For seeds of delight sprout in wild, bright array!

Luminescent Dreams

In a night full of giggles, the moon wears a grin,
As dreaming raccoons invite everyone in.
They ride on the beams of star-sprinkled snow,
While fireflies gather to put on a show.

With each twinkle of laughter, the cosmos does sway,
As pillows hold meetings on funny things to say.
A blanket of chuckles, so cozy and light,
Wraps round all the wishes, so playful, so bright.

The dreamscapes are filled with a silly parade,
Where cupcakes wear hats, and the lemonade's made.
In this land of the wacky, all giggles take flight,
Unraveling joy in the cool, starry night.

So come share the whimsy, the glow of delight,
In dreams that are buzzing with laughter so bright!
Together we'll float on this whimsical stream,
And dance through the night in our luminescent dream!

Illuminated Pathways

Frogs wearing crowns on lily pads,
Pondering why the road is so mad.
Bright fireflies dance in silly parade,
While owls crack jokes in the evening shade.

Bouncing bunnies with hats too tight,
Debate the stars in a shimmery light.
Chasing shadows, they tumble and fall,
Laughing so loud, they wake up the mall.

Jellybean trees grow sugary vines,
With squirrels rapping on new wooden signs.
The raccoons laugh at their own silly pranks,
As the moon giggles in silvery flanks.

Giggling grasshoppers play peek-a-boo,
With flowers that tickle and call out 'Woohoo!'
In this whimsical world, joy knows no end,
Every path is a joke, every twist a friend.

The Blossom of Possibility

A pickle in a tutu sways in the breeze,
Dreaming of waltzing with tall, swaying trees.
Daisies wear sunglasses, looking quite cool,
While bees throw a dance party right by the pool.

Toasters unite, with bread in a rush,
Making up new recipes without any hush.
'Challah' or 'Sourdough?' they ponder and shout,
As the muffins just giggle and roll all about.

Fluffy clouds wear smiles, so bright and unbent,
They sail through the sky, on pure laughter sent.
A kite sparks joy, with colors that blend,
Tails tied in knots, but this won't be the end.

Bubbles blowing bubbles, it's quite the affair,
Floating up high without a single care,
In this garden of whimsy, dreams sprout and twirl,
Every petal unfolds a fantastical whirl.

In the Shade of Wisdom

Socks on the roof know wise old tricks,
With backyard debates on their favorite picks.
The wise old owl wears spectacles tight,
As he offers advice in the moon's gentle light.

A mischievous fox pens a quirky book,
On the art of stealing—take a closer look.
His secrets unfold in a comically way,
Even the tortoise has something to say.

Squirrels arguing over the best nut,
While an acorn laughs, stuck in a rut.
In a world where common sense often takes flight,
The absurd is the norm, and the funny feels right.

Birds crafting jokes that are oddly profound,
While flowers all giggle, their laughter abound.
In the shade of wisdom, where nonsense is king,
Life's silly moments are the best kind of bling.

Nature's Resurgence

A cactus with arms that can tickle and hug,
Claims it's the star of the National Rug.
With humor so sharp, it makes others grin,
Declaring the prickling is 'just a big win.'

Raccoons in pajamas raid the kitchen,
Practicing moves for their dance floor mission.
They shimmy and shake with their spoons on the sly,
Challenging veggies to join in the high fly.

Sunshine pours down like a syrupy treat,
While daisies do cartwheels, skipping with feet.
In this lively garden, each creature will show,
That mirthful revival puts on quite the show.

A wind chime orchestra plays 'Over the Moon,'
As frogs form a band, hoping to croon.
In this resurgence, each laugh takes a stand,
Nature's a party with humor so grand.

The Symphony of Being

Life's a tune, a silly jig,
We dance along, so free and big.
Each step a laugh, a quirky beat,
A melody that can't be beat.

With every note, we surely play,
We'll sing and joke our cares away.
A symphony of joy and cheer,
Our laughter ringing far and near.

Clumsiness our finest art,
Imperfect moves that steal the heart.
So join the band, let spirits rise,
In this grand farce, we claim the prize.

Life's ridiculous, a light ballet,
In this circus, we'll find our way.
With giggles loud, we're on a spree,
Composing life with humor's key.

New Buds of Thought

Ideas bloom from silly seeds,
In wacky minds, they sprout like weeds.
A thought can tickle, twist, and turn,
With every chuckle, watch them burn.

Take a moment, let jokes fly,
Like butterflies up in the sky.
Each giggle's spark, a chance to grow,
New buds burst forth, a vibrant show.

From dreams so wild, they start to sprout,
Random musings, there's never a drought.
Twirling up thoughts with flair and fun,
Our laughter's song has just begun.

So pluck the fruit from humor's tree,
Savor the zest of glee, oh me!
With quirky quirks and playful tone,
We'll plant our seeds, make whimsy known.

Beyond the Canopy

Beneath the branches, life's a jest,
Where giggles grow and never rest.
We swing like monkeys, oh what fun,
In this enchanted, silly run.

With hiccups loud and snorts so bright,
We'll sneak a peek at pure delight.
Exploring worlds of giddy dreams,
Beyond the trees, it always seems.

The woods are filled with playful shouts,
As letch we sing of life's funny bouts.
A tapestry of whimsy's weave,
In endless laughter, we believe.

So join the blunders, take a chance,
We'll stir the air with funny dance.
Together here, we weave and play,
In the shade, let joy lead the way.

The Palette of Emotion

A splash of giggles, hues of glee,
Paint all your feelings honestly.
With every brush, a grin composed,
Life's canvas is humorously disposed.

Twists of purple, splashes of joy,
Crafting laughter, oh what a ploy!
With strokes so wild, we dab and see,
Colors of life, bright as can be.

Each shade brings forth a chuckle's charm,
Creating warmth within the calm.
A palette rich with wild-eyed fun,
Where stories live and hearts are spun.

So dip your brush in life's bright hues,
Create a mural with your views.
Together we'll paint the world anew,
In every shade, let joy shine through.

www.ingramcontent.com/pod-product-compliance
Lightning Source LLC
Chambersburg PA
CBHW071851160426
43209CB00003B/506